TALKIN' DIRTY

by

Copyright 1989

Ozark-Maid Candies
5857 Osage Beach Parkway
Osage Beach, Missouri 65065
1-573-348-2202
ozarkmaid@gmail.com

About "TALKIN' DIRTY" . . .

This book is not one filled with vulgarity. The title **"Talkin' Dirty"** means the very simple and graphic expressions used by many rural people. This book contains phrases and expressions of country people which I have remembered and collected over many years.

Farmers and other rural folks live a simple life & learned to express their thoughts and emotions with a graphic regional speech that is both rich and colorful. This simple life influenced them to use few words to communicate, but to do it in such a way as to put their point across in a very vivid and picturesque way.

For instance, to express Boredom they might say: **"That's 'bout like watchin' grass grow."**; Feeling Out Of Place: **"I felt like a bastard at a fam'ly picnic."**; Nervousness: **"I'm jumpier'n a whole truckload a' starvin' kangaroos."**; or Mentality: **"He's dumb as a box a' rocks!"**

Country people have a way of creating instant mind pictures with such vivid and colorful expressions as: **"That dress you're wearin' is 'bout as sexy as socks onna' rooster."**; or **"Her rear-end looks like two tomcats fightin' inna' gunnysack."**

There is much wisdom in these sayings, such as: **"Straddlin' th' fence (neutrality) is th' same as straddlin' th' middle of th' road."** (might get hit from both sides) or: **"Why should a man buy a cow if he gits th' milk free?"** (why marry?) or: **"Marryin' a gal just 'cause she's pretty is th' same as buyin' a house 'cause it's gotta' good paint job."**

Many of these sayings do have some crude words in them, but the intent is not to be vulgar, but to place more emphasis on some things.

The purpose of this book is two-fold. First, I would like to see these colorful expressions preserved. They are part of our heritage. Secondly, I compiled this for your enjoyment, and I sincerely hope you do enjoy.

I really do appreciate your buying this book. I will just say, as we country people say, **"I thank you 'till yer' better paid."**

— LES BLAIR

Note: I would appreciate hearing from you, and receiving your comments and suggestions, — even contributions for future books. Better still, if in my part of the country, stop by and say **"Howdy"**. My address is:

Ozark-Maid Candies
5857 Osage Beach Parkway
Osage Beach, Missouri 65065
1-573-348-2202
ozarkmaid@gmail.com

INDEX

Subject	Page
ABODE, — SIZE, NEATNESS, LOCALE	4
ACTIONS, — PHYSICAL	5
ADVICE, ADMONITION	6
AGE	7
AMBITION, ENERGY, LAZINESS	7
APPEARANCE, — CLOTHING	9
APPEARANCE, — FEATURES	10
APPEARANCE, — GENERAL	10
APPEARANCE, — LOOKS, UGLY, ETC.	12
ATTITUDE	13
CAPABILITY	14
CHARACTERISTICS, — PHYSICAL	15
CHARACTER, — BAD	17
CHARACTER, — GOOD	19
CHARACTER, — UPBRINGING	19
CLEANLINESS	20
COMPARISONS, — GENERAL	20
DEATH, DYING	21
DIFFICULTY	22
DISTANCE	23
DUPLICITY, GULLIBILITY	23
EATING, — HUNGER, THIRST	24
EGO	25
EXPERIENCE, KNOWLEDGE, MENTALITY	26
EXTRAVAGANCE, STINGINESS	29
FEELINGS, — EMOTIONS	30
FEELINGS, — JOY, ANGER, FEAR	31
FEELINGS, — NERVOUSNESS	33

Subject	Page
FEELINGS, — PHYSICAL	33
FOOD QUALITY	34
FRIENDSHIP, FRIENDLINESS	35
HEALTH	35
HUMOR, HUMOROUS	37
INTOXICATION	37
LIES, LIARS	38
LUCK	38
MONEY	39
OBESITY, THINNESS	39
PROMISES, THREATS, ORDERS	40
RELATIONSHIPS, — GENERAL	42
RELATIONSHIPS, — MALE, FEMALE	43
RELATIONSHIPS, — WEDLOCK, FAMILY	45
RESPONSIBILITY	46
SANITY	47
SPEECH, TALKING, LISTENING	48
STATEMENTS, — GENERAL	51
STATUS, — ACHIEVEMENTS	51
STATUS, — ECONOMIC	52
SUCCESS, FAILURE, — GENERAL	54
TEMPERAMENT	57
TIME	58
TROUBLES, PROBLEMS	59
WEATHER, NATURE	61
WORTH, USEFULESS	61

ABODE, — SIZE, NEATNESS, LOCALE

"Our town is so small, we hafta' take turns bein' th' town drunk." (humorous exaggeration of size of town)

"Our house wuz so small you cud'n't cuss a cat 'thout gittin' hair in yore mouth."

"Her house is so dirty, — she pro'bly hasta' wear a flea collar 'round her ankle."

"Our house wuz reel small, — we even had to go outside to change our minds."

"Thet room is so cluttered you cud' lose a thrashin' machine in it."

"A cow cud'n't find her own calf in that house." (it was cluttered, messy)

"I lived catty-wampus 'cross th' holler." (lived at an angle across hollow, — not directly across)

"I live where th' hoot-owls roost with th' chickens an' th' women cut th' wood." (humorus for: rural, sparsely populated area)

"I live back in th' boon-docks (or boonies)." (in a rural, woodsy sparsely populated area)

"We lived in country so rough, if you got sick an' th' weather was bad, they'd hafta' let you die an' git you when it faired up." (humorous saying)

"We live in what I call a 'poke 'n plumb' town, — you poke yer' head out th' window an' yer' plumb outta town."

"There ain't no hooks on th' floor!" (said to family members throwing clothing on floor)

"Your room is messy, — looks like a pig-pen!"

"We got no more privacy than a goldfish!" (none whatsoever)

"Th' town we live in is just a wide place in th' road." (jokingly said of small town)

ACTIONS, — PHYSICAL

"**You walk like you gotta' ketch in yer' git-a-long.**" (it looks like you have a limp)

"**Yer' slower'n sorghum molasses onna' cold day in January.**" (you move or act very slowly)

"**He's quicker'n a jackrabbit.**" (he is very quick, with mind or actions)

"**He blinks like a toad inna' hailstorm.**" (blinks his eyes very often)

"**Keep yer' head up an' yer' tail out like you owned th' place.**" (show confidence, don't be shy)

"**He shook like a dog shittin' peach seeds.**"

"**He kin throw a rock a country mile.**" (has a very good throwing arm)

"**She was dancin' up a storm.**" (she is a very good (or very active) dancer)

"**He sneaks 'round like a chicken thief.**" (quietly and furtively moves about)

"**She walks like an ol' hen with a egg broke inside.**" (she has a strange walk)

"**He runs like a chicken pullin' a wagon.**" (he's got a strange kind of run)

"**He walks like he's gotta' corncob up his rear.**" (he's got a stiff-legged walk)

"**She walks funny, — like a chicken in high oats.**" (a bobbing, high stepping walk)

"**We're afoot, — we gotta' hoof it.**" (we have no car, we have to walk)

"**She waddles like a duck.**" (she walks with a waddle)

"**Don't put anything in yer' ear 'cept yer' elbow.**" (don't stick things in your ear)

ADVICE, ADMONITION

"Seems we allus' give advice by th' bucket, an' take it by th' grain."

"You'd better cool yer heels for a while." (it would be best if you waited)

"You'd best cultivate yer' own garden." (you need to attend to your own affairs)

"Shhh! Little pitchers have big ears." (careful what you say, the kids are listening)

"You cain't put one foot in two shoes at one time." (can't take two positions, or — do your job and others at same time)

"If'n a frog had wings, he wud'n't whomp his butt when he landed." (said in response to useless wishing)

"Go soak yer' head in buttermilk." (take time to calm yourself, cool down)

"If you butcher a prime hog, you kin use ever'thing 'cept th' grunt an' squeal." (with quality, you get more use out of it)

"See a pin & let it lie, — you'll need a pin 'fore you die." (old saying — save things, they will come in handy at some time)

"Never wuz a lane that didn't have a turnin.' " (things will always change, for better or worse)

"Call a spade a spade an' dig with it." (don't complain, make do with what you have)

"Don't cut off yer' nose just to spite yore face." (don't do or say something which you will regret)

"Don't start choppin' 'till you've treed th' coon." (don't jump to conclusions or get ahead of yourself)

"If you cain't stan' th' heat, git outta' th' kitchen."

"Yer' gonna' hafta' learn to quit suckin' eggs!" (humorous, — you need to start taking action sooner, — quit hesitating)

AGE

"**Yer' still wet behine' th' ears.**" (you are very young, or inexperienced)

"**That feller wuz born old.**" (appears old, by actions or attitude)

"**She ain't no spring chicken.**" (she is getting old)

"**Why, you're older than dirt!**" (humorously said of another's age)

"**I reckon I've run 'round th' pot after th' handle longer than him.**" (I am older than he is)

"**There ain't no fool like an old fool.**"

"**Ole age ain't bad, — when you think 'bout yer other choice.**" (when you think of death)

"**He's as old as th' hills!**"

AMBITION, ENERGY, LAZINESS

"**He's too lazy to holler "sooey"**if'n th' hawgs wuz eatin' him up." (that is really lazy)

"**As lazy as you are, you'd better marry a feller that'll give you a personal maid.**" (you don't do anything for yourself or others)

"**Yer' as lazy as th' dog that leaned 'gainst th' wall to bark.**"

"**He's allus' suckin' a hoe handle.**" (lazy — leaning on tools, doesn't work very often)

"**He mus' have callus's on his butt.**" (very lazy — sits around)

"**Have you gotta' broken arm?**" (can't you do that yourself?)

"**He don't care if school keeps 'r not.**" (he is lazy and not concerned)

"**Whats time to a hawg?**" (time doesn't matter to one who is lazy or unconcerned)

"**You'll never set th' world on fire.**" (you will never accomplish much at the rate you are going)

"**I'm fulla' piss an' vinegar.**" (I am full of energy, ready to go)

"**I'm busier'n a one-armed paperhanger.**" (too busy to take on anything else)

"**I'm busy as a one-legged man at a ass-kickin.'** " (I am really busy)

"**He's like a chicken, scratchin' fer what he's got.**" (he is endevoring to achieve his goal)

"**You cain't be in six places with one behind.**" (you can't do everything yourself, or be in more than one place)

"**He don't let no grass grow under his feet.**" (he keeps moving foward, striving to achieve his goal)

"**She kin reelly make th' fur fly.**" (she is a good worker or, uses a lot of energy in her endevors)

"**He's got his fingers inna' lotta' pies.**" (involved in many businesses, or endevors)

"**You gotta' keep yer' nose to th' grindstone.**" (keep trying to achieve your goals)

"**He's kinda' like a blister, — don't show up 'til th' works all done.**"

"**You gotta' keep yer' mouth open a long time before a roast duck flies into it.**" (don't wait for things to come, — go after them)

"**She wuz runnin' 'round like a chicken with its head chopped off.**" (very busy)

"**When oppurtunity knocks, you gotta' git up offa' yer' butt an' let it in.**"

"**I'm busier'n a two-tailed cat.**"

"**He's reely work brittle.**" (willing to work hard)

"Yep, he's gonna' take up books." (he is going to start school or college)

"He wuz workin' up a storm." (working hard)

APPEARANCE, — CLOTHING

"Yore clothes fit tighter'n a first day bride's hind-end." (your clothes are too tight)

"That dress looks like it's 'bout to eat you up." (that dress is too tight and exposes too much)

"That new suit makes him look like a mule inna' buggy harness." (he looks different or out of place in that suit)

"Wal, you won't be a swinger any more." (jokingly said of man with new jockey shorts)

"That dress you're wearin' is 'bout as sexy as socks onna' rooster." (decidely not sexy looking)

"Yer'pants 'r reely baggy, — looks like you're smugglin' rice outta' China."

"I don't like th' color a' that dress, — it's kinda' turd muckle dun." (very drab)

"That feller's wearin' his high-water pants." (wearing pants too short)

"He's a rag'lar clothes-horse." (wears very good clothing)

"Yer' barn door's open, an' yer' horse is gonna' git out." (your fly is unzipped)

"You shore are gussied up." (you are dressed up, — you look nice)

APPEARANCE, — FEATURES

"His eyes is closer together than a' earthworm's." (very close-set eyes)

"Don't be lookin' at me with them hawg-eyes." (don't look at me with those reproachful or begging eyes)

"Don't look at me with them hang-dog eyes!" (with those sad or begging eyes)

"They look like two peas inna' pod." (look like twins)

"His eyes stuck out so far, you cud' rope them with'a grape vine." (bug-eyed)

"Yer' wearin' too much lipstick, yer' mouth looks like a chicken's ass in pokeberry time."

"Yew look like sum'body just kicked yore dog!" (you have a very sad or depressed look)

"He looks like he's been hit in th' face with a wet squirrel." (a disheveled or surprised look)

"That gal's gotta' complexion like peaches an' cream." (a very nice complexion)

"Yore face is redder'n a turkey's hind-end in pokeberry time." (face is flushed or sun-burned)

"I see you gotch'er ears lowered." (you have a new haircut)

APPEARANCE, — GENERAL

"She looks like 40 miles a' bad road." (looks bad, from sickness or other reasons)

"She's common as pig tracks." (very plain looking)

"**You look like death warmed over.**" (you really look terrible, — look sick)

"**You just cain't tell from th' looks of a toad how high he'll jump.**" (you can't judge what a person can do by his appearance)

"**You look bright-eyed an' bushy-tailed this mornin.'** " (you look vibrant and ready to go)

"**Beauty is only skin deep, but ugly is clear to th' bone.**"

"**You do look perky today!**" (you look happy, or — look like you are feeling good)

"**She's as freckled as a turkey egg.**" (lots of freckles)

"**He was naked as a jaybird.**" (not wearing anything)

"**She wuzn't wearin' a stitch!**" (she was naked)

"**Why're you grinnin' like a 'possum eatin' bumble bees?**"

"**She looks like she's been rode hard an' put away wet.**" (she looks exausted or sick)

"**That feller looks like he might last thru' just one more clean shirt.**" (he looks like he is very sick)

"**Don't judge a book by it's cover.**" (the appearance of a person will fool you)

"**She's brown as a berry.**" (she has a very good tan)

"**You look like th' tail end a' hard times.**" (you look very sloppy, — wearing poor clothing)

"**There they were, standin' there like eggs inna' carton.**" (side by side)

"**It won't ever be noticed onna' gallopin' horse.**" (not perfect, but looks good enough)

"**Thar he wuz, grinnin' like a skunk eatin' cabbage.**"

"**How cum' yer' grinnin' like a wave on a slop bucket?**"

"**He wuz grinnin' like a cat eatin' cockleburrs.**"

APPEARANCE, — LOOKS, UGLY, ETC.

"He's so ugly, he hasta' tie a bone 'round his neck to git th' dog to play with him!"

"She's ugly as a mud fence after a hard rain." (she is very plain looking)

"He's so ugly, he hasta' sneak up onna' glass a' water just to git a drink."

"I wud'n't take her to a dog fight, — even if'n she had a chance to win!" (she is extremely ugly)

"He looks like he's been beat with a ugly stick." (he's ugly)

"He's gotta' bad case of th' uglies."

"She's ugly 'nough to stop a' eight-day clock!"

"She's as plain as dried mud."

"She's so ugly, she'd make th' train take a dirt road."

"She's too ugly to lay on th' beach, — th' tide wud'n't even come in."

"He's as ugly as homemade sin."

"He's so ugly, he hasta' slap his-self to sleep."

"He (or It) is as ugly as yesterday."

"She's plain as home-made soap." (she has very common looking features)

"That's as ugly as shit onna' barn door."

"That kid wuz so ugly when he wuz born, thet th' doctor slapped his mom."

ATTITUDE

"Yer' 'bout as much fun as havin' jock itch!" (that is no fun at all)

"You're 'bout as subtle as a shovel fulla' crap." (not subtle at all)

"I 'spect he'll just sit on th' fence." (he will not take a position on the matter)

"You're kin 'spect to git rode if'n you make an ass outta' yer'self."

"Don't ever look a gift horse in th' mouth." (don't be suspicious of someone's generosity)

"He's hard as nails." (he is very stern, demanding)

"You want yer' cake an' eat it too." (you want more than you deserve)

"Th' water that's past don't turn th' mill wheel." (don't look back, look to the future)

"Don't muddy up th' well you git water frum." (don't be ungrateful to your benefactor)

"Just wait, — in time th' grass becomes milk." (have patience)

"I'd ruther drag a board than do that." (that does not appeal to me at all)

"I'd ruther watch grass grow than do that." (that would bore me very much)

"You need to fish 'r cut bait." (quit being indecisive)

"She's bold as brass." (she is very foward)

"Don't put up yer' umbrella 'fore it rains." (be positive in attitude)

"He made no bones 'bout it." (was very frank, forthright)

"She's so contrary, cheese wud' make her have th' trots." (said in jest to illustrate one's contrary attitude)

"Yep, that's his pet peeve, an' he pets it reel often."

"That gal wud' make a horse laugh." (always cheerful, funny)

"You gotta' take th' fat with th' lean." (be positive when negative things happen)

"I'll jest dance with who brung me." (I will stick with a prior decision)

"Don't carry yer' shotgun at half-cock." (don't go with a chip on your shoulder looking for trouble)

"You'd complain even if you wuz hung with a new rope." (you would complain no matter what you had)

"Straddlin' th' fence is 'bout like straddlin' th' middle of th' road." (liable to be hit from both sides)

"Why, I'm just as reg'lar as a goose-a-goin' barefoot." (I am very regular in my endeavor)

"I believe you wud' go to a goat-ropin.' " (you enjoy to go places)

"I shore hope you ain't done a perm'nent job a' makin' a fool outta' yer'self."

"You put me in mind of a snotty-nosed youngan.' " (your attitude reminds me of a very immature child)

CAPABILITY

"He kin fertilize th' whole field with just one a' his farts."

"Yer' not able to say boo to a goose!" (you are inept, have little or no ability)

"That feller's kinda' Jack-of-all-trades." (has ability to do many jobs, is very handy)

"You cain't teach a old dog new tricks." (one does not change much after reaching a certain age)

"You kin teach a old dog new tricks, — you just don't want to see him doin' them!." (older people should act in a mature way)

"A pint cain't hold a quart." (some people have only so much ability or capability)

"You just cain't see th' wood fer th' trees." (you are looking beyond, you can't see the things right in front of you)

"Three people kin keep a secret if two of them're dead."

"You cain't use two onna' broom." (no help wanted or needed with housework)

"Th' teacher caught me, — She mus' have eyes in th' back of her head." (she does not miss anything)

"She cud'n't carry a tune inna' bucket with th' lid on." (a very poor singer or musician)

"She reelly does things up in brown rags." (she does things nicely or well)

"She sews with a hot needle anna' gallopin' thread." (she is an excellant seamstress)

"I cain't turn off work like I used to." (can't accomplish as much as when younger)

"He cud' sell you a anvil even if you wuz treadin' water." (he is a very good salesman)

"He cud' sell two milkin' machines to a farmer with one cow, and then take th' cow as a downpayment." (a top-notch salesman)

CHARACTERISTICS, — PHYSICAL

"Why, he's big 'nough to go bear huntin' with a switch." (humorous: appears big enough to fight a bear with bare hands)

"She ain't no bigger'n a minute." (she is a very small, or petite person)

"He'd be a lot taller if'n he didn't have so much turned under." (he has very large feet)

"He's 'bout knee-high to a grasshopper." (he's short, or small)

"He's growin' like a bad weed." (growing rapidly)

"That feller cud'n't hit his rear end with both hands." (he is very uncoordinated)

"He cud'n't lead geese to water with a double rein." (he is very clumsy)

"He's like a bull inna' china closet." (very clumsy)

"You cain't hit a bull in th' ass with a bass fiddle." (you are very clumsy, inaccurate)

"Thet mare's reelly inbred, — why, she's her own grandma!"

"Wal, that's a good family horse." (a long-backed horse)

"He's blind as a bat at high noon."

"He's deaf as a door."

"She looks like a bale of hay that's had it's string busted." (spreading out some, or pregnant)

"He's gotta' neck as long as a well rope." (he has a neck that is much longer than normal)

"I bet he could eat corn on th' cob thru' a picket fence." (he has teeth that protrude noticeably)

"She traded her fat behine fer a bird's bottom an' got th' legs that went with it." (a scrawny behind and bird-like legs)

"If somebody says "haul ass", he'd hafta' make two trips." (he has a very scrawny and small rear end)

"He's so bowlegged he cud'n't ketch a hawg in a ditch."

"She's shore built fer speed." (she has a slender figure)

"She's gotta' rear end like a forty-dollar mule." (nicely shaped bottom)

"She's shore gimlet-assed." (she has a very small bottom)

"He's got hands as big as hams."

"**Her rear end looks like two tomcats fightin' inna' gunny sack.**" (she has a bulging & moving rear end)

CHARACTER, — BAD

"**You cain't make a silk purse outta' a sows ear.**" (can't make good or successful person if traits not right)

"**He's slipperier'n a' eel inna' tub fulla' snot.**" (he is very tricky or evasive)

"**He's so crooked they'll haf'ta screw him in th' ground to bury him.**" (he is very dishonest)

"**He's crooked 'nough to steal pennies offfa' dead man's eyes.**" (very dishonest)

"**He's so durn crooked he cud'n't sleep inna' round house.**" (he is very dishonest)

"**He's as sneaky as a weasel inna' chicken house.**" (he is very untrustworthy)

"**That feller is too narrow 'tween th' eyes.**" (humorous saying to indicate one can't be trusted)

"**He's learnt to howl by runnin' with th' wolves.**" (he was influenced to turn bad by keeping wrong company)

"**He's got all th' qualities of a dog 'cept loyalty.**" (not even as good as a dog)

"**He's as low as a snakes belly inna' wagon rut.**" (he is a bad one, — no good)

"**He's a ring-tailed tooter with his tail screwed in.**" (wild and uncontrollable)

"**I'd trust him 'bout as far as I cud' sling a bull by th' tail.**" (I don't trust him at all)

"**He's not worth th' bullet it'd take to shoot him.**" (he is really worthless)

"**He's lower'n a dawg's belly.**" (he hasn't got many or any good qualities)

"He's on'ry as a egg-suckin' hound." (he is really mean)

"He's lower than whale crap!" (very unsavory & bad character)

"He's lower'n a mole's bellybutton on diggin' day." (has little or no worthwhile qualities)

"It's seems like it's always th' weeds that grow th' best." (dishonest people appear to prosper)

"He's reelly gone to th' dogs." (did have better qualities, but has turned bad)

"Give'm an inch, an' he'll take a mile." (bad character, will take advantage of you)

"A rotten apple kin spoil th' whole barrel." (one of bad character can influence others for bad)

"It's hard fer' a empty bag to stand upright." (one with few or no good qualities will not be liked or repected)

"That feller will do to watch." (bad reputation, dishonest in some way)

"Anyone that wud' run 'way with you wud' drop you at th' first lamppost." (would have poor judgement and poor character)

"You jest cain't make a silk purse outta' a sow's ear." (not possible to make a fine person if one lacks certain qualities)

"He's orn'rier than cat manure." (he is very mean)

"He's meaner'n a chicken-eatin' sow." (he is an extremely cruel or dishonest person)

"If'n you lay with th' dogs, you'll end up gittin' fleas." (you will be influenced for bad by keeping bad company)

"Aw, he never did keer if'n he farted 'r blew a tin whistle!" (he had no concern for others or his own actions)

"Left her? That's just good riddance t' bad rubbish!" (he was worthless, she is better without him)

"He's got th' sex life of a' rabbit, — jumpin' from hole t' hole." (he has no morality)

"**He ain't got 'nough guts t' say boo t' a goose!**" (he has no courage whatsoever)

CHARACTER, — GOOD

"**That feller plows a straight furrow.**" (he is honest man)

"**Ain't she sum'thin', — one of th' ol' blue hen's chicks.**" (a neat or good person)

"**He's shore earned his place in Heaven.**" (is a good Christian)

"**Pretty is as pretty does.**" (it is'nt your status or looks, but what you are & do that counts)

"**Yep, he's a diamond in th' rough.**" (though unrefined, he has very good qualities)

"**She's th' toppin' on th' cake. She's th' whipped cream on th' pie.**" (she's someone very special)

"**His heart is in th' right place.**" (he is a good man, kindhearted)

"**He shore has gotta' lotta' gumption.**" (he has a lot of courage)

CHARACTER, — UPBRINGING

"**Th' apple don't fall far from th' tree.**" (you will act as you are raised by your parents)

"**Water seeks its own level.**" (you will act as you are raised)

"**Th' breed is stronger'n th' pasture.**" (parentage is stronger than surroundings)

"**A tree falls like it leans.**" (person turns out like he was raised)

"**Blood's thicker'n water.**" (parentage is strong influence)

"**Never wuz a good knife made outta' bad steel.**"

CLEANLINESS

"Yer' so dirty that yer' not fittin' to 'sociate with hawgs."

"That feller looks like he's been chewin' tobaccy an' spittin' agin' th' wind."

"He smells strong 'nough to stink a dog offa' gut wagon." (he has a very strong body odor)

"He stinks bad as a dead dog inna' rain barrel." (he really stinks bad)

"It's as clean as a hound's tooth." (it's very clean)

"He smelled bad 'nough to gag a maggot!" (he needed bath, had a very strong body odor)

"You ain't fittin' to 'sociate with hogs!" (you are too dirty even for the company of pigs)

"Yer' black as a pot." (that is very dirty)

"Wash behine' yer' ears, you cud' grow 'taters back there." (humorous saying, generally use by mothers)

COMPARISONS, — GENERAL

"Now, that stands out like a big diamond inna' goat's ass." (it really shows up)

"Wal, that beats a dry hackin' cough." (humorous saying for: not bad, better than nothing)

"That beats a poke in th' eye with a sharp stick." (that will do, better than nothing)

"That's rough as a corn cob." (a bad situation or an uneven surface)

"That fishin' line is fine as a frogs hair."

"That feller's fast, quicker'n a jackrabbit."

"Aw, it's six a' one anna' half-dozen of 'nother." (doesn't really make any difference, they are basically the same)

"It wuz noisier'n two skeletons makin' love onna' tin roof."

"That wuz some fire, — wud' make hell look like a lightnin' bug." (exaggeration to stress it being a very large fire)

"Why, that's flat as a pancake."

"That went offa' him like water offa' duck's back."

"It's quieter'n a mouse pissin' inna' ball a' cotton." (it is very quiet)

"That's as natural as a hog eatin' slop." (something certainly to be expected)

"Yer' blind as a goose!" (can't see things right in front of your face)

"That's soft as a baby's butt." (very soft)

"That's th' best thing that happened since sliced bread!"

"That's as handy as a' pocket onna' shirt!"

"That's 'bout like settin' th' house on fire t' roast a' chicken." (doing something drastic that accomplishes little)

DEATH, DYING

"I wuz reelly sorry to hear that he'd cashed in his chips." (sorry to hear he had died)

"He ain't livin', — too scared of dyin.'" (fear of death is hampering his life)

"It's dead as yesterday's dishwater." (a dead issue or object)

"He's dead as a doornail."

"Poor feller, he's on his last legs." (he is near death)

"I hear he's 'bout to kick th' bucket." (he is about to die)

"He looks like he might last thru' just one more clean shirt." (he appears to be very near death)

"Old age ain't too bad, considerin' th' alternative." (considering death)

DIFFICULTY

"Wal, it don't take long to curry a small horse." (won't take long, it's a small job)

"That's 'bout like pushin' a wheelbarrow with rope handles." (an extremely difficult task)

"You cain't get there frum here." (humorus saying to show difficulty in giving directions to a place)

"Thats 'bout as easy as lickin' honey offa' thorn tree." (a difficult thing to do)

"That's 'bout as easy as pickin' fly dung outta' black pepper." (that is a very difficult task)

"Now, don't put yer'self out none." (don't go to too much trouble)

"Don't make a mountain outta' a molehill." (don't make it more difficult)

"That'll be like lookin' fer a needle inna' haystack." (very difficult)

"That'll be like nailin' Jello to th' wall." (almost impossible task)

DISTANCE

"Yep, we live 'bout half-a-quarter down that road." (taken from land measurement, — about ⅛ mile)

"We live just a hawk'n a spit down th' road." (we lived very close by)

"Th' Jones live just a hoot'n a holler away." (they live just a short distance away)

"We live a pretty fur piece frum here." (we live a pretty far distance from here)

"He lives within spittin' distance." (he lives very close)

"You betcha' it's close, — just a stones throw from here." (a short distance)

"We wuz w'thin a shout a' bein' home." (we were close)

DUPLICITY, GULLIBILITY

"He bought a pig inna' poke on that deal." (he was misled on that transaction, or business deal)

"I smell a skunk!" (I am very suspicious of this situation (or business deal)

"She's done a good job a' butterin' him up." (making him feel good for her own reasons)

"She reelly gave him th' horse laugh." (she deceived him and was not sorry about it)

"I bet he's playin' 'possum." (acting as if asleep or dead, — acting as if dumb on business deal)

"Aw! Yer' pullin' my leg." (you are trying to fool or mislead me, or lying to me)

"**You're tryin' to steal my thunder.**" (you are trying to take credit for my accomplishments)

"**Now, don't be sheddin' no crocodile tears.**" (acting sympathetic, with other motives)

"**He's holdin' with th' hounds, an' runnin' with th' hare.**" (being a false ally to both sides)

"**He's laughin' up his sleeve.**" (he has deceived or got the best of someone)

"**Watch that feller, he'll hornswoggle you.**" (be careful, he will cheat you or take advantage of you)

"**He shore saw him comin.'** " (he cheated or bested him in that deal)

"**Why, butter wud'n't melt in her mouth.**" (she says complimentary things she does not mean for purposes of her own)

"**Now, that ain't th' whole piece of cloth.**" (that is not the complete story)

EATING, — HUNGER, THIRST

"**We usta' eat so many turnip greens, we hadta' wear coal-oil rags 'round our ankles to keep th' cut-worms off.**" (humorous)

"**Thanks, no more food fer me, — I'm full as a tick!**"

"**I've ate so much, I feel like a poisoned pup!**" (I feel bloated)

"**That dawg's so full you cud' crack a tick on his belly.**" (a full and tight stomach)

"**My belly thinks my throat's been cut.**" (humorous saying meaning: I am very hungry)

"**I'm hungry 'nough to eat a stink bug off'n a dead skunk.**"

"**Feedin' you puts me in mind a' sloppin' a hawg!**" (you have the appetite and manners of a pig)

"I'm hungry 'nough to eat buzzard's bait."

"He wuz hungrier'n a wolf."

"I'm hungry 'nough to eat th' south end of a skunk goin' north."

"I cud' eat a horse, — hoofs an' all!" (I am extremely hungry)

"He's th' tall hawg at th' trough when it cum's to eatin.' " (he eats more (or faster) than anyone else)

"Fingers wuz made b'fore forks." (excuse for using fingers to eat with)

"Yer' gonna' eat us outta' house an' home." (you have a very large appetite)

"Don't eat standin' up, — you cud' git fat legs." (don't snack, sit and eat regular meals, or you will put on weight)

"He's th' runt of th' litter; — musta' had to suck hind tit." (humorous saying: — small, must have not got enough to eat)

EGO

"She thinks she' a dab onna' stick." (she is extremely vain, has a high opinion of herself)

"Her nose is stuck up so high in th' air, I bet she'd drown if'n it come a hard rain." (snooty, — thinks she's better than others)

"A feller thet toots his own horn never gits tooted." (praise yourself, and nobody will praise you)

"She's awful persnickety." (she is extremely particular and picky)

"If I cud' only buy him for what he's worth an' sell him for what he thinks he's worth." (has extremely high opinion of himself)

"Th' sun don't just rise an' set 'round you." (you are not as important as you think)

"Met anyone today that you liked better than yer'self?"

"When a fellers' head swells up, his brain stops workin.' " (a feeling of self-importance will cloud one's thinking)

"Fools' names an' fools' faces, are often seen in public places." (a very old saying)

"She's one'a them high-brows." (she is stuck up, snooty)

"He thinks he's th' biggest frog in this puddle." (he has a very large ego)

"Don't git to thinkin' yer' a big wheel, — you know that sum' mighty little dogs pee on sum' awful big wheels!"

"I'd shore hate to pay his taxes if they wuz based on what he thought he wuz worth."

"You mus' think yer' th' top dog in this here kennel." (you think you're pretty important)

"He thinks he's th' head honcho." (self important)

"You cain't find a big 'nough hat for that head." (too much ego, big-headed)

EXPERIENCE, KNOWLEDGE, MENTALITY

"I don't think his porch lite' is on." (he doesn't have much brainpower)

"She's duller than ditch water." (not much thinking power)

"He ain't got sense 'nough to pound sand inna' rathole."

"She puts two an' two together an' gits five."

"He's dumb as a box of rocks." (that's dumb)

"She's dumb as dirt!" (she's pretty dumb)

"He ain't got sense 'nough to cum' in outta' th' rain."

"He's duller'n a widder woman's axe." (doesn't have much brain power)

"**If brains wuz dynamite, he wud'n't have 'nough to blow his nose.**" (very little brains)

"**If'n you even had a brain, you'd have it in yer' hand playin' with it.**" (no common sense)

"**Better git outta' th' sun b'fore it boils th' water in yore head.**" (humorous saying implying more water than brains)

"**You don't know doodley-squat!**" (you know nothing)

"**It come to me like a bolt outta' th' blue.**" (it occured to me suddenly)

"**He don't know crap from wild honey!**" (he is dumb)

"**She knows as much 'bout that as a dog does 'bout Sunday.**" (knows nothing about that)

"**She wuz hid behine th' door when brains wuz passed out.**" (she does not have much brainpower)

"**He's dumber'n a barrel of hair!**" (very dumb)

"**That's like th' blind leadin' th' blind.**" (the teacher or leader has no more knowledge than the student or follower)

"**You ain't got th' sense that God gave a goose!**"

"**Close th' door! — Wuz you born inna' barn?**" (don't you have good manners or sense?)

"**He's dumb as a post.**"

"**Dogs ain't too smart, — just look at th' way they greet each other.**"

"**He's reelly dumb, — thinks Price-Waterhouse is a pay toilet.**"

"**You think I got these bumps on m' head by fallin' offa' turnip wagon?**" (humorous saying: smarter than you give me credit for)

"**His Ma musta' dropped him on his head when he wuz a baby.**" (his thinking is impaired)

"I know all th' answers, but nobody asks me th' questions."

"He don't know his ass from a hole-in-th-'ground."

"He's gotta' head fulla' feathers." (light in brains, low thinking power)

"Give that feller a shovel, an' he wud' ask you fer th' directions." (not much practical sense)

"A peck a' common sense is worth a whole bushel a' learnin.' "

"Mos' peoples hinesight is twenty-twenty."

"He don't know straight up from apple butter." (knows very little or nothing)

"Two heads 'r better'n one, — even if one is a sheep's head." (a good natured slur on the other person)

"Yer' as dull as stump-water." (very low learning ability)

"Yer' a real air-head!" (very little brains)

"She cooks her peas 'n turnips in th' same pot." (she's inexperienced)

"He's green as a gourd." (he's very inexperienced)

"He's still wet behine th' ears." (young, inexperienced)

"You cud' go to th' ocean an' not find water." (very inexperienced or incapable)

"Wal, you live an' learn."

"I didn't just ride in onna' load a' 'taters, you know." (you can't fool me, I'm not gullible)

"So, now it's th' egg teachin' th' chicken." (one inexperienced giving advice to one experienced)

"You don't know nuthin', — don't know cum' here from sic 'em." (very inexperienced or dumb)

"Don't ask him, — he don't know shit from Shinola!" (it's useless to ask, — he doesn't know anything)

EXTRAVAGANCE, STINGINESS

They're reely puttin' on th' dog." (being extravagant, making a show of their money)

"Sum' folks make a dollar an' spend a dollar anna' dime." (they spend beyond their income)

"She likes to puddle in high cotton." (live higher than her means)

"I'd like to have their recipe for high livin.' " (don't understand how their standard of living is so high)

"Stingey? Why, that feller is so tight he'd skin a flea for th' hide an' tallow."

"He's 'bout as tight as a bull's rump in fly-time." (he is extremely stingey)

"He's wud'n't give a dime to see th' Resurrection." (he is extremely stingey)

"He's as tight as a frog's hind end."

"She's tighter'n bark onna' tree." (she is extremely stingey)

"He'd sell a dozen eggs an' borry one back fer breakfust." (he is a very stingey man)

"She's as tight as last winter's long johns." (very close with her money)

"He's closer with money than a tie-game."

"She's so tight she squeaks when she walks." (is extremely stingey)

"They're allus' tryin' to keep up with th' Jones'es." (being extravagant, spending beyond means)

"He's reelly a high roller." (he lives lavishly, spends lot of money)

FEELINGS, — EMOTIONS

"**I wud'n't walk a mile to see a piss ant eat a whole bale a' hay!**" (I am not excited, or don't get excited easily)

"**We ain't had this much excitement since th' hogs ate little brother.**" (humorous)

"**We ain't had this much excitement since Ma got her tit caught in th' wringer.**"

"**That shore wuz a shot in th' arm.**" (that elated me, made me feel better)

"**As th' preacher said, — you gotta' wrassle deep in yore guts.**" (to feel something deeply)

"**I'm tellin' you, I felt like a bastard atta' fam'ly picnic.**" (felt very much out of place or unwelcome)

"**Wal, I'll be a suck-egg mule.**" (saying of surprise)

"**I cud'n't stand it any longer, — I was like a drunkard smellin' whiskey thru' th' jail-house door.**" (couldn't resist temptation)

"**He wuz standin' naked 'fore th' Lord.**" (people knew everything, nothing left to hide)

"**You just don't lift my skirts high 'nough.**" (not excited about what you said or did)

"**I'm just like a graveyard, — I'll take anything.**" (I will accept what comes my way)

"**I'm feelin' awful sorry this mornin.'**" (I am feeling very depressed, or sick)

"**I'm as comfortable as a snake's belly inna' old wagon rut.**" (I am satisfied with my economic status, or position)

"**I'm cool as a cucumber.**" (I am not agitated)

"**I'm as contented as cows inna' corn field.**" (got all I need, content with life)

"**I feel like I been sent for an' cud'n't come.**" (depressed, or ailing)

"**I feel lower'n a mole's bellybutton on diggin' day.**" (depressed, or sick)

"**You're actin' awful twittle-pated.**" (confused)

"**It shore makes a diff'runce if you gotta' dog in th' race.**" (more interest in contests/sports if friends/relatives competing)

"**That weighed heavier on me than a tail fulla' cockleburrs.**" (was a burden, bothered me greatly)

"**That's 'bout as excitin' as watchin' clothes dry.**" (very dull)

"**That's 'bout as much fun as watchin' grass grow.**" (boring)

"**I'd ruther drag a board.**" (not looking foward to something)

"**She was just a-cryin' an' a-snubbin.**" (a sobbing cry)

FEELINGS, — JOY, ANGER, FEAR

"**That gal wuz so excited, she had'ta walk sideways just to keep from flyin.'**"

"**She wuz walkin' on air!**" (she was very excited, happy)

"**She's ever' bit as cross as a ol' settin' hen.**" (she's very cranky and fussy)

"**Thet feller shore rubs me th' wrong way.**" (he irritates me)

"**We jawed up a patch.**" (had a quarrel or argument)

"**That is th' las' straw.**" (I have lost all patience)

"**I'm as happy as a clam at high tide.**" (I am very content at this time)

"**'Thout a doubt, that's th' best thing that's happened since sliced bread.**" (humorous saying to indicate pleasure)

"**Happy? Yep, he wuz as happy as a hawg inna' mud wallow.**" (thought life was great)

"**He's happier'n a dog inna' meat-packin' house.**" (thought things couldn't be much better)

"**You'da thought he had th' world by th' tail.**" (very happy with his lot in life)

"**I'm mad 'nough to chew splinters.**" (very angry)

"**He was rompin' an' stompin' like a hungry dog.**" (he was in a rage)

"**He reelly flew off th' handle.**" (lost temper, went into a rage)

"**She shore got his nanny goat.**" (she sure confounded or upset him)

"**Hatin' is kinda' like burnin' down yer' house to kill a rat.**" (hate is destructive)

"**There ain't no love lost between us.**" (we dislike each other)

"**I'm so dern glad to be home, it made me glad I went.**"

"**Now, wud'n't that boil yer' pot?**" (wouldn't that make you angry?)

"**I wuz so mad, I could've just spit!**"

"**That'll shore git his nanny-goat!**" (that will make him irritated, or mad)

"**I just felt like runnin' 'round yellin' with my apron over my head.**" (I felt very frustrated, angry)

"**She's 'fraid of her own shadow.**"

"**That rascal reelly took to his heels.**" (ran off scared)

"**He reelly gits in my hair.**" (he irritates me, makes me angry)

"**I wud' bet that he dirtied his britches.**" (I would bet he was very scared)

"**Just hold yer' water, — don't go gittin' mad!**"

FEELINGS, — NERVOUSNESS

"I'm as nervous as a porcupine inna' balloon factory." (extremely nervous)

"She's jumpier'n a whole truck-load a' starvin' kangaroos." (very nervous and jumpy)

"He's as nervous as a June bride inna' feather bed."

"He's as nervous as a long-tailed cat inna' room fulla' rockin' chairs."

"She's reelly nervous, — just one step ahead of a fit." (near a nervous break-down)

"I was as nervous as a two-bit whore in church."

"She's reelly gotta' bee in her bonnet." (she is excited, elated, or nervous)

"I felt like a fish outta' water." (out of place, nervous)

"I wuz as nervous as a Flamenco dancer with weak kidneys." (very nervous)

"Don't put to sea inna' storm." (calm down before you act)

"Now, don't git yer bowels inna' uproar." (calm down, don't get upset)

FEELINGS, — PHYSICAL

"As tender as a gum boil onna' crocodile." (it hurts)

"I'm dry 'nough to spit cotton." (I am very thirsty)

"I'm snug as a bug inna' rug." (I am comfortable)

"I'm dryer'n a popcorn fart." (I am very thirsty, or dry)

"I'm cold as a well-diggers hind-end in Alaska." (I am very chilled)

"I'm colder'n a ol' maid in January."

"Colder'n a witch's breast inna' brass bra onna' freezin' day in January."

"I'm hot'ern a billy goat inna' pepper patch." (I am over-heated)

"I'm as dry as a goat's butt in March." (I am very thirsty)

"I'm cool as a cucumber." (I am not hot)

"I'm dry as powder." (I am thirsty, or - I'm not wet)

"I'm just 'bout done in." (exausted or broke)

"I feel 'bout like a bar of homemade soap after a hard washday." (very tired)

"I'm fresh as a Daisy." (I feel good and am ready to go)

FOOD QUALITY

"This hen is so tough you cud'n't stick a fork in'er gravy." (very tough meat)

"She'd burn water tryin' to boil it!" (a very bad cook)

"Thet gal shore sets a fine table." (she's a good cook)

"This here soup mus' be warmed over! — You cud'n't hev' got it thet hot in one heatin'!"

"This soup cud'n't be any hotter if it'd cooked all day."

"Her coffee wuz so weak you cud' stand inna' barrelful an' see yore toes."

"That's fox-huntin' coffee." (good & strong)

"That tasted awful! — 'bout lik Ole Woodsman flydope strained thru' a snot-rag." (jokingly said to stress bad flavor)

FRIENDSHIP, FRIENDLINESS

"**An ounce a' help is better'n a whole pound of preachin.'**"

"**Wal, you shore are a sight fer sore eyes!**" (greeting showing pleasure at seeing them)

"**I'm plum' proud an' pleased to see (or meet) you!**" (a common saying when meeting or seeing someone)

"**I thank you 'til yer' better paid.**" (I will simply say thanks until I can return the favor)

"**We've howdied, but we ain't shook.**" (we know each other by sight but have not been formally introduced)

"**She didn't know me from Adam's off ox.**" (we hadn't met or she didn't recognize me)

"**What pleases you just tickles me to death.**"

"**You know th' latchstring is always out.**" (you are always welcome)

"**He's as friendly as a speckled pup.**" (he is extremely friendly)

HEALTH

"**You cain't put scrambled eggs back inta' th' shell.**" (there is some deterioration or damage to the body that can't be repaired)

"**I'm so low, I'd hafta' use a step-ladder to kick a duck in th' hine-end.**" (sick, or broke)

"**Poor Suzie, she's got one foot in th' grave.**" (her health is very bad)

"**You oughta' hev' seen it, — he bled like a stuck hog.**"

"**Jed's been kinda' under th' weather.**" (health has not been very good)

"What's th' matter, Dearie, hev' you got a risin'?" (have you got a boil, or swelling?)

"How'm I? — Aw, just fair to middlin.' " (not feeling as good as usual)

"I feel like a moose had a miscarriage in m' head." (I really got a bad headache, or hangover)

"I'm feelin' awful sorry this mornin.' " (I am feeling very sick)

"I feel as low as a snake's belly inna' wagon rut." (sick, or very depressed)

"I've got twinges in m' hinges." (I have arthritis)

"I feel lower'n a dog's belly." (I feel sick, or depressed)

"I'm feelin' lower'n a mole's bellybutton on diggin' day." (I am feeling sick, or depressed)

"I feel like I been rode hard an' put away wet." (I feel exausted or sick)

"I gotta' ketch in m' git-a-long." (I'm having trouble with my hips, or legs)

"I feel like I been sent for an' cud'n't come." (I feel exausted or sick)

"I feel like I've been run thru' a wringer." (exausted, emotionally down or sick)

"I feel like I've been chewed up an' spit out." (exausted or sick)

"I'm fit as a fiddle." (in good shape)

"I'm sick'ern a dog." (I am very sick)

"Don't worry 'bout feelin' good, — you'll git over it."

"I'm stiff as a board."

"She wuz feelin' awful poorly." (she was very sick)

"I'm kind'a down in m' back." (ailing)

HUMOR, HUMOROUS

"**Here's yer' hat, — what's yer' hurry?**" (humorous remark made to one leaving)

"**If you cain't be good, — be careful.**" (humorous advice, — if you are going to have sex, avoid having kids)

"**Sex wud' be a lot more fun if hav'in' kids wuzn't included as a penalty.**"

"**Why did I marry her? We just gotta' lotta' faults in commom.**"

"**Naw, we don't hev' any kids, — I won't even touch her coffee!**"

"**Lean over, an' I'll slip you a slobber.**" (give you a kiss)

"**Yer' hair? Just rake it, pile it, burn it, — an' start over.**" (humorous saying)

INTOXICATION

"**He'd git drunk if you hit him in th' tail with a rotten apple.**" (easily intoxicated, no capacity for alcolholic beverages)

"**He's awful bad to drink.**" (he is probably an alcolholic)

"**He's so drunk he's plumb whomper-jawed.**" (his jaw is slack)

"**He drinks like a fish.**" (is probably an alcoholic)

"**She ended up bein' drunk as a hoot-owl.**"

"**I'd ruther meet a fat man on th' super-slab than a drunk.**" (I would rather meet a over-eater than drinker on freeway)

"**I wuz drunker'n a skunk.**" (very drunk)

"**Jake wuz three sheets to th' wind.**" (he was drunk)

"**He wuz drunker'n a coon on stump likker.**" (he was very drunk)

LIES, LIARS

"Th' only way you cud' become a bigger liar is if you'd put on weight."

"A windy ain't a lie 'less you tell it fer th' truth."

"Always tell th' truth, even if you hafta' lie to do it."

"I'd lie to you only if I cud'n't tell you th' truth severul diff'runt ways."

"That feller lies so much he hasta' have his wife call th' dog." (even the dog won't believe him)

"That's a lotta' baloney." (I do not believe that)

LUCK

"If he fell inta a pile of crap, he wud' come up smellin' like a rose." (he is very lucky)

"That kid has bad luck, — his yo-yo pro'bly don't even cum' back."

"He's awful unlucky, — if he had a pet rock, it wud' pro'bly wet on his leg."

"With his luck, he wud' pro'bly ketch th' bouquet at a funeral."

"If'n you threw him in th' river, he'd cum' up with a fish in his mouth." (he is very lucky)

"Tawk 'bout bein' unlucky, he's self-employed an' still got fired' " (said in jest)

MONEY

"Money's kinda' like a pile of manure, no good 'less it's spread 'round."

"You cain't git blood outta' a turnip." (you can't get money out of someone who doesn't have it)

"There's a chance a' ruinin' yer' friends mem'ry if you loan him sum' money."

"If I had his money, I'd throw mine away."

"She worships th' awlmighty dollar." (she is greedy for money)

"He's got more money than a porcupine's got quills." (he is very rich)

"He's got 'nough money to burn a wet mule!" (and that takes a lot of money)

OBESITY, THINNESS

"She's reelly skinny, — pro'bly hasta' stick her tongue out for you to see which way she's goin' "

"She's awful scarce-hipped." (she's very thin)

"She's so skinny that she hasta' walk by twice to make a shadow."

"That feller is too thin to cast a shadow."

"He's fatter'n a town dawg." (a town dog is one that everyone feeds and is usually very fat)

"She's ate sum' 'taters an' they've settled in one place." (she's fat in the bottom)

"She's thinner'n a bat's ear."

"She's two axe handles wide in th' behine." (she's wide across the bottom)

"She's spread out like a cold supper." (she's very wide and fat)

"She's skinny as a plucked chicken." (she is very underweight)

"He's so thin you'd hafta' to shake th' sheets to find 'em."

"She's thin 'nough to take a bath inna' gun barrel." (she is painfully thin)

"That feller is so thin you cud' paint stripes on 'em an' use 'em for a yardstick."

"That gal is heavier'n a ton of lard inna' molasses can." (she's very fat)

"She'll never git wrinkled, — ever see wrinkles onna' balloon?" (humorous way of saying she is fat)

"She'd be more spic if she had less span." (she would look better if she lost weight)

PROMISES, THREATS, COMMANDS

"I'm gonna' kill that kid, an' tell God he died!" (said tongue in cheek out of frustration)

"I'm gonna' give 'em a dose of his own medicine." (I will repay him in kind, — vengence)

"Quit pesterin' me er I'll slap you bald-headed!"

"I'll be there if nothin' don't break ner cum' untwisted." (if nothing happens)

"It'll be a cold day in July b'fore I do that agin!" (I will not do that again)

"I'm gonna' smack a skillet fulla' crap outta' you!"

"I'm gonna' box yer' ears!" (I am going to slap you!)

"I'm gonna' be on you like flies on poop!" (threat of disciplinary action)

"Stop that cryin', — er I'll give you sum'thin' to cry about!" (reason to cry, — a spanking or slap)

"Do that agin' an' I'll whup you w'thin a inch of yore life!" (a very sound spanking)

"Just watch it, er I'll cut yer' water off!" (be good, or I will dicipline you)

"Don't pester me er I'll turn you ever' way but loose!" (don't aggravate me or I will discipline you thoroughly)

"Yep, I'm gonna' do it even if it harelips all th' hawgs in Texas." (I am determined to do it no mattter what happens)

"Aw, if that wuz to happen, I'd eat my hat!" (said to express disbelief of an event happening)

"B'fore I'd do thet, I'd git a tin bill an' peck shit with th' chickens."

"I'm gonna' kick his ass up 'tween his shoulders!"

"Quit sassin' me er I'll slap th' snot right outta' you!"

"I'm gonna' give you what-fur!" (discipline you thoroughly)

"Don't do thet, er yer' name'll be mud." (you will be in trouble)

"If you'd do thet for me, I'd dance at yer' weddin' inna' pig trough." (I will be grateful if you do that)

"I'm gonna' kick yer' ass so hard, — you'll hafta' fart thru' yer' collar!"

"Will you quit beatin' 'round th' bush?" (quit delaying, get to it)

"Just foller your nose!" (look!, it is right in front of you)

"Quit that lolly-gaggin' 'round!" (stop loafing)

"Use yer' snot rag!" (wipe your nose with your handkerchief)

"You shoo-fly now, 'fore I swat you!" (get away from me)

"**Don't give me no sass!**" (don't talk back to me)

"**When she sez' "frog", — I jump!**" (humorous for: she is the boss)

"**Don't let th' door hit you in th' ass!**" (get out, — leave)

"**Don't git th' cart b'fore th' horse.**" (do it right)

"**You better make haste slowly.**" (take time to do it right)

RELATIONSHIPS, — GENERAL

"**Don't keep a fire for an enemy, — you'll git burnt.**" (don't hate someone who has wronged you, it will hurt you)

"**Yep, he got fried in his own grease.**" (he got hurt by circumstances of his own making)

"**You ought'a been there, — I'm tellin' you, all hell broke loose!**" (there was considerable conflict)

"**I'm gonna' take that feller down a peg er two!**"

"**We ought'a let'm stew in his own juice.**" (let him try to get himself out of problems of own making)

"**Good fences makes for good neighbors.**" (a farmers saying, — keep fences mended so your stock doesn't bother neighbors)

"**I gotta' bone to pick with you!**" (you have offended me)

"**I wuz reelly on th' wrong end of th' stick on that issue.**" (I took the wrong side)

"**We ought'a let'em go at it tooth n' nail.**" (let them fight it out)

"**He warts me 'til I cain't stand it.**" (he irritates me greatly)

"**She reelly told him how th' cow ate th' cabbage.**" (she berated him soundly)

"**He wuz caught 'twixt th' devil an' th' deep blue sea.**" (in a situation hard to get out of)

"**Ma, you gave him th' lions share!**" (gave him more)

"She (or he) turned him ever' way but loose!" (big fight)

"Two wrongs don't make a right." ("getting even"or revenge is not the answer)

"Wal, I cain't kill you, — there's a law agin' it." (tongue in cheek saying when aggravated)

"He orta' be worked over with a piss-ellum club!" (deserves a beating)

"He's shore got his stinger out for that feller." (was angry and vengeful with him)

"Yep, they went 'round an' 'round on that." (had a big disagreement)

"Him an' that banker are hand in glove." (they are closely associated)

"We all stand naked in our clothes." (we are all alike)

"If yer' in yer' neighbor's melon patch, don't tie yer' shoe." (avoid suspicious circumstances)

"Yep, they're thick as fiddlers in hell." (close relationship)

"A little oil helps to save sum' friction." (kind words help)

RELATIONSHIPS, — MALE & FEMALE

"Men (or Women) are all alike, — They just have diff'runt faces to tell them apart."

"Why buy a cow if yer' gittin' th' milk for free?" (why marry her if she is going to sleep with you regardless?)

"A feller don't chase a streetcar he's awlreddy caught." (his interest may wane if she is too easy)

"She leads him 'round by th' nose." (she dominates him)

"If you don't have sum'thin' fer sale, don't advertise it." (don't be foward unless you really want a sexual relationship)

"**She put's me in mind of a wild mare goin' to stud.**" (she has sex on her mind, has loose morals)

"**He's gettin' a little somethin' on th' side.**" (he is having an affair with another woman)

"**If you want'a go out with him, you gotta' break th' ice.**" (make the first move or overture)

"**He's been sowin' his wild oats, then prayin' for crop failure.**" (humorous: been sleeping around, hoping hasn't fathered children)

"**She's tryin' to git inta his britches.**" (she is trying to have sex with him)

"**He wants to jump her bones.**" (he wants to go to bed with her)

"**He's got th' "hots"fer her.**" (he is aroused sexually by her)

"**He shore knows his way 'round th' hen-house.**" (he is quite a ladies man)

"**He's makin' calf-eyes at you.**" (he is very infatuated or in love with you)

"**A hot love soon turns cold.**" (a relationship built on passion alone will not last)

"**For ever' Jack there's a Jill.**" (there is always someone who you can love and have a relationship with)

"**If you love me, you gotta' love my dog.**" (humorous saying)

"**She fell head over heels in love.**"

"**He shore likes you, — takes to you like a hawg after persimmons.**" (he likes you very much)

"**He went south onna' load of logs.**" (he left for greener pastures rather abruptly)

"**I feel sorry for her, — she drove her ducks to a poor market.**" (she is in a bad relationship or marriage)

"**She's (or He's) not th' only pebble on th' beach.**" (there will be other women (or men) in your life that you can care for)

"**He's (or She's) not th' only fish in th' sea.**"

"Where cobwebs grow there comes no beau." (old saying, — if you are sloppy or slovenly, you are not likely to attract anybody)

"I'm feelin' purty unhandy with him." (we are not having a good relationship, not gitting along)

"She's gotta' be a reg'lar saint to put up with him." (she is a very good and patient person to endure him)

RELATIONSHIPS, — WEDLOCK, FAMILY

"They jumped over th' broom-stick." (they took the big step and got married)

"They split th' blanket." (they became separated or divorced)

"She's kinda' like an ol' hen with one chick." (hovering over, spoiling)

"I hear that he jumped th' traces." (I hear he has left his wife)

"They've got kids from Widlum to Wadlum 'thout a space b'tween." (they have lots of kids, close together in age)

"He's in th' doghouse agin.'" (his wife is angry with him again)

"More kids? I wud'n't give a nickel for 'nother one, — wud'n't take a million for any I got." (love my kids, but we got enough)

"It'll be hard to break him to halter." (going to be difficult for him to settle down to marriage)

"That pore young'un is a wood's colt." (that poor child was born out of wedlock)

"Keepin' yer' hubby in hot water ain't gonna' make him any tenderer." (fussing with him will not make him any more loving)

"He's a real butter n' egg man." (he is a good provider)

"That dern fool must think a new match'll light his fire." (thinks new women will turn him on more sexually)

"Poor feller, — he shore is hen-pecked." (dominated by wife)

"She's been married so many times, she's got veil rash."

"Don't ever marry fer money, — it's a dern sight cheaper to borry' it."

"They had a whole passel a' kids." (they had a very large family)

"Marryin' a gal just 'cause she's pretty is 'bout th' same as buyin' a house just 'cause it's gotta' good paint job."

"Oh, oh, he's got sum' war paint on." (married man with lipstick smear on collar)

"That boy is allus' holdin' onto her apron strings." (spoiled, momma's boy)

"My young'ans 'er goin' to be a comfort in my ole age, but they're gonna' help me reach it faster, too!"

"When my wife sez "frog", I jump." (humorous saying, — she gives the orders)

"She wears th' britches in that family." (she rules family)

RESPONSIBILITY

"You'd lose yer' head if it wuzn't tied on." (you are very irresponsible)

"You've made yer' bed, now lay in it!" (you caused your own troubles, deal with them yourself)

"Yer' chicken'll cum' home to roost." (you will be responsible for your actions)

"I'm burnin' my bridges behind me." (made decisions, will stick to them, win or lose)

"Now, that's th' pot callin' th' kettle black." (both are equally guilty)

"You gotta' paddle yer' own canoe." (depend on own resources)

"He dirtied his own nest." (he is responsible for his problems)

"**I cain't mess with that, — I got other fish to fry.**" (I have other more pressing problems)

"**I kin bear just 'bout anything, — if it ain't my fault.**" (we do not like to accept blame for troubles)

"**Th' only excuse for not bein' here is to call in dead, — an' you kin only use that one once!**"

"**Th' road ta hell is pave with good intentions.**" (intending to not enough, — you must do it)

"**You'd better take th' bit in yer' own teeth.**" (you had better take charge)

"**Wal, you gotta' bite th' bullet.**" (face consequences of your actions)

"**What crawls under yer' belly'll land on yer' back.**" (will reap results of your actions)

"**When push cum's to shove, you'll hafta' do it.**" (it is your responsibility)

"**I figure he'll fly th' coop.**" (run away from his responsibility)

"**Now, you ain't got no call to do that.**" (not required to (or shouldn't) do that)

SANITY

"**I believe he's gone 'round th' bend.**" (he has become insane)

"**I don't think he's got both oars in th' water.**" (he's not completly sane, or rational)

"**His elevator don't go all th' way to th' top.**" (not completely rational, slightly crazy)

"**He's a crazy a a peach orchard boar.**" (he's insane)

"**He's crazy as a shit-house rat!**" (extremely crazy)

"**He's missin' a few shingles from his roof.**" (slightly crazy)

"'Pears like he don't have 'nough studs for his drywall." (seems to be short of brainpower or rationality)

"He's a few bricks short of a load." (lacking in his head, — either brains or rationality)

"He's a half-bubble off plumb (or center)." (mind isn't right)

"He's got bats in his belfry." (he is crazy)

"That feller is mad as a March hare."

"He's crazy as a June bug."

"She wuz a mite tetched." (a little crazy)

"He ain't playin' with a full deck." (not quite sane)

"She don't have alla' her marbles." (somewhat crazy)

SPEECH, TALKING, LISTENING

"Tell me, — I'm all ears." (I am interested and listening)

"Go 'head, lay it on me." (go ahead, talk, you have my attention)

"I'd ruther talk to a post." (not responsive)

"Don't swallow th' bull an' leave th' tail hangin' out." (don't believe an unlikely story without investigation)

"A feller that toots his own horn don't ever get tooted." (praise yourself, and others will not praise you)

"What's th' matter, — cat got yer' tongue? (why are you silent?)

"You ain't listenin', — it's goin' in one ear an' out th' other." (you are not absorbing what I am saying)

"We jawed up a patch." (talked a lot)

"She cud' talk th' leg offa' chair." (she talks a lot)

"Now, fill yer' pipe with that, — an' smoke it." (think about what I've said)

"Now here's a bone for you to chew on." (something for you to think about)

"That gal's gotta' voice like a buzz saw on cast iron." (a man's voice, gruff & raspy)

"She's gotta' tongue that wags at both ends." (she talks a great deal)

"She cud' talk yer' arm off." (humorous, — she loves to talk)

"Empty cans make lotsa' noise, — th' same goes for empty heads." (can say a lot that means nothing)

"When that feller opens his mouth, — his brain shifts inta' neutral." (doesn't think about what he is saying)

"She told him how th' cow ate th' cabbage!" (she berated him very soundly)

"Her tongue is loose at both ends." (she has an uncontrollable tongue, talks too much)

"I've told you a million times not to exaggerate!" (humorous saying)

"That preacher shore is long-winded." (preachs long sermons)

"Quit beatin' 'round th' bush." (say what you mean)

"She let th' cat outta' th' bag there." (let a secret slip out)

"He's tellin' another cock 'n bull story." (an exaggerated or untruthful story)

"You spend too much time talkin' from th' teeth out." (you don't think about what you say)

"Heifer dust is what gals say when they mean bullshit."

"She swears like a fish-wife." (she uses too much profanity)

"That preacher's stopped preachin' an' started meddlin.' " (his sermon made me feel guilty)

"Talkers most times ain't do'ers."

"Just who rattled yore cage?" (who asked you to talk?)

"That preacher should learn t' measure his sermons by depth, — not length!"

"I'd take th' comp'ny of m' dog over thet woman, — his tail wags 'stead a' his tongue." (she talks too much)

"You need to quit hollerin' down th' rain barrel." (you need to quit wasting time on useless talk)

"Th' squeaky hinge gits th' grease." (don't be shy, speak up for what you want)

"He kin cuss th' gate plumb off it's hinges." (he's got a very foul mouth)

"Now, there's a feller that kin start th' bull rollin.' " (very talkative, not always truthful)

"A closed mouth ain't gonna' catch any flies." (words can't harm you if not spoken)

"Now there's a real wind-bag!" (one who is prone to talk too much)

"Who pulled yer' chain?" (who asked you to talk?)

"Just 'tween you an' me an' th' bedpost." (keep what I am about to tell you a secret)

"Wal, talk of th' devil." (humorous saying: arrival of someone)

"You took th' words right outta' m' mouth." (I was about to say the same thing)

"Taste yer' words b'fore you let 'em past yer' mouth." (think before you speak)

"Put yer' brain in gear b'fore engagin' yer' mouth." (think before you speak)

"Don't make a mountain outta' a molehill by addin' dirt." (don't add to a problem with gossip)

"You've got th' saw by th' wrong tree." (you are telling story wrong, or doing that wrong)

"She cud' talk yer' arm off, then cuss you out for bein' crippled." (humorous reference to one who talks a lot)

STATEMENTS, — GENERAL

"**Don't throw out th' baby with th' bath-water.**" (don't discard everthing, keep the worthwhile portions)

"**Don't choke onna' gnat an' swallow a camel.**" (don't object to minor fault, and then accept larger one)

"**You shore hit th' nail on th' head there.**" (what you did (or said) is correct)

"**Why, that's just as plain as th' nose on yer' face.**" (it is very apparent)

"**That knife is so dull you cud' ride to town on it.**"

"**If that wud'n't take th' warts offfa' toad.**" (I am very surprised)

"**You cain't beat that with a switch.**" (that is great, — just right)

"**If that don't beat a hen a-peckin.'** " (that is great, or — I am surprised)

STATUS, ACHIEVEMENTS

"**Most knockin' is done by people that don't know how to ring th' bell.**" (ridicule comes from people who can't or won't succeed)

"**You like th' apples more if you hafta' shake th' tree.**" (you appreciate things more if gained through honest labor)

"**I'm gonna' kill two birds with one stone.**" (accomplish more than one thing with one endevor)

"**He pulled their chestnuts outta' th' fire.**" (he got them out of trouble)

"**Every dog has his day.**" (most will, regardless of status, have some accomplishments)

"**You'd better leave well 'nough alone.**" (be satisfied with things as they are)

"Tall trees ketch a lotta' wind." (people in command get criticism)

"If you want yer' place in th' sun, you gotta' expect sum' blisters." (if in limelight, will get friction and criticism)

"You gotta' climb th' mountain to see th' view." (it takes effort for reward)

"He's got more cows (or money, etc) than Carter's got little liver pills."

STATUS, — ECONOMIC

"You cain't fall outta' a well." (can't be any worse off, no matter what happens)

"They're 'bout to th' end a' their rope." (in very dire circumstances)

"He's so pore he cud'n't buy hay for a night-mare."

"Pore people have pore ways." (poor people have to learn to do with much less)

"Thats life! — if it ain't chicken, — it's feathers." (it's either good times or bad)

"Seems like it's either feast 'r famine with us." (good times or bad)

"He's reelly ridin' th' gravy train." (is very successful)

"Our roof leaks a little, but we allus' let comp'ny sleep inna' dry spot." (we don't have much, but we share it with others)

"I'm so pore that I cain't even pay attention."

"They wuz pore as Job's turkey, — hadta' lean on th' fence to gobble."

"They wuz so pore they ate th' wallpaper." (humorous saying, — had very little food)

"She wuz pore as a outhouse mouse." (she was extremely poor)

"Our ground wuz so pore you cud'n't raise a row with a pitchfork." (soil was rocky, infertile)

"If yer awlreddy down, how kin you fall?" (can't get any lower)

"Bein' pore ain't no disgrace, — but it shore is unhandy."

"Beggers cain't be choosers, that's for sure."

"They been livin' from hand to mouth." (they have a very bare existance)

"We cain't hardly make ends meet." (we never have enough money)

"Wal, it's th' chicken neck or nothin.' " (we are in hard times)

"He is as pore as a church mouse."

"Yep, he's doin' good, — got th' world by th' tail with a down-hill pull." (he's very successful)

"Yep, I'm doin' right well, — reely eatin' high on th' hawg." (very successful)

"They're eatin' in high clover." (they are doing very well)

"He's choppin' tall cotton." (he is doing very well, is successful)

"It's allus' th' weeds that grow th' best." (it appears that many bad people prosper)

"Bein' pore, we had t' eat a lotta' jam san'wiches, — two pieces a' bread jammed together!"

"If I had yer' money, I'd throw mine away!"

SUCCESS OR FAILURE, — GENERAL

"**All them gover'ment bureaus n' political jobs 'er like a septic tank, — all th' reelly big turds rise to th' top.**"

"**My campaign wuz a bust, — went over like a lead balloon.**" (a very definite failure)

"**He reelly bit th' dust.**" (failed miserably)

"**He went off th' deep end.**" (gambled & failed)

"**His goose is cooked!**" (he is ruined)

"**Just milk th' cow, — don't pull off th' udder.**" (take your share, don't be greedy)

"**Don't count yer' chickens b'fore they're hatched.**" (don't count on success before it comes)

"**There's more'n one way to kill a cat than by chokin' him on hot butter.**" (humorous saying: another way to accomplish that)

"**Don't bawl over spilt milk, — just find yer'self 'nother cow.**" (don't complain, — pick yourself up and try another way)

"**Don't cry over spilt milk, there's water 'nough in it awlready.**" (it doesn't help to complain about what has happened)

"**It's dog-eat-dog.**" (it's very competitive)

"**Better keep yer' fingers crossed.**" (hope for success)

"**I'm gonna' go th' whole hog!**" (I am going to put all my effort and resources into it)

"**You're gonna' git scalded on thet deal!**" (you are going to get hurt on that deal, — don't do it)

"**Th' Oprey ain't over 'til th' fat lady sings.**" (don't give up too soon, try until there is no hope)

"**A miss is as good as a mile.**" (it has to be successfull (or exact), or it is of no value)

"**Th' ol' sow got an acorn.**" (someone got a small victory).

"He shore bought a pig inna poke!" (he sure came out on the bad end of that deal)

"I hope you don't lay an egg." (I hope you don't fail)

"He reelly crapped in th' oatmeal." (he really made mess of things)

"He got left holdin' th' bag." (came out loser, more than others)

"Yep, I got done, — just by main strength an' akwardness." (I did it, but it took much perserverance)

"If you burn yer' tail, you just hafta' set on th' blister." (accept the results of your own mistakes)

"He got burnt on that deal." (he lost on that deal)

"Don't worry, I know which side m' bread is buttered on." (I know who my benefactor is, and will act accordingly)

"Don't put all yer' eggs in one basket." (don't gamble all your resources on one venture)

"He's gonna' feather his own nest." (going to do things which will benefit himself)

"Don't kill th' goose that lays th' golden eggs." (don't do harm to something that benefits you)

"Wal, let th' chips fall where they will." (I will accept whatever comes)

"He may laugh outta' th' other side of his mouth." (he may regret his actions or decisions)

"Just keep in mind that th' feller that laughs last, — laughs best." (may prove to be successful)

"It'll all come out in th' wash." (things will come out for the best eventually)

"Thet shore upset his apple cart." (that really spoiled his plans)

"He won't win, — got no more chance than a grasshopper inna' chickenhouse." (no chance whatsoever)

"He's got as much chance as a head 'thout a chicken." (he has no chance of success)

"He'd last 'bout as long as a paper shirt inna' bear-fight." (he would fail quickly)

"There ain't no place too high for a jackass loaded with gold to reach." (people can buy a top position with enough money)

"Now, don't be countin' yer' chickens b'fore they'r hatched." (don't think or claim success until you actually have it)

"I gotta' tell you, you're reelly skatin' on thin ice." (you are taking a big gamble)

"You cain't win, ner break even, — you cain't even quit th' game." (humorous saying)

"This ain't horseshoes, — close don't count!" (must do it right)

"If wishes wuz horses, beggars wud' be ridin.' " (it does no good to just wish for something)

"Th' post allus' wears out b'fore th' hole." (need to continue to put effort into something)

"There's more'n one way to skin a cat." (more than one way to accomplish a goal)

"Call a spade a spade an' start diggin.' " (accept what you have and use it to accomplish your purpose)

"Yer' gonna' hafta' use elbow grease." (you are going to have to work hard)

"You gotta' make hay while th' sun shines." (do things today, don't put off, to be successful)

"You'd better look b'fore you leap." (investigate well before jumping into a venture)

"You gotta' git up one time more'n you fall." (you need to persevere, always try again after set-back)

"Stoppin' at third base don't add no more to th' score than strikin' out." (don't give up, — persevere)

TEMPERAMENT

"Yer' as subtle as a shovel fulla' crap."

"You'd complain if you wuz hanged with a new rope." (you are never satisfied with what you have)

"Th' squeaky hinge gits th' grease." (yell or complain enough and you get results)

"She's as cranky as an ol' settin' hen." (grouchy and fussy)

"You've gotta' mouth fulla' "gimmies"." (always wanting something)

"Yer' 'bout as funny as a rubber crutch." (you are not amusing)

"He's like a hawg on ice." (he goes all sorts of directions, doing as he pleases)

"You kin ketch more flies with honey than you kin with vinegar." (a gentle manner is better than an abrasive one)

"He ain't fit comp'ny for man 'er beast." (he is cranky, surly or hard to get along with)

"You musta' got up on th' wrong side a' th' bed." (you are out of sorts, cranky, irritable)

"Don't worry, his bark is a lot worse'n his bite." (he is not nearly as mean as he sounds)

"Wal! She's on her high horse!" (belittling others, snooty)

"You wud' try th' patience of a iron saint!" (you would irritate anybody)

"He mus' be a blockhead, with that chip on his shoulder."

"He's as cranky as a grizzly bear with a sore ass!" (he is very irritable)

"You ain't got no couth!" (you are uncouth)

"You'd argue with a post!" (you tend to be argumentative)

"She cud' make people happy by just lettin' 'em alone." (has an irritating mannner)

57

"Yer' as mule-headed as you kin be!" (very stubborn)

"Yer' stubborn as a mule!" (very stubborn)

"He's allus' gotta' rule th' roost." (be boss (top rooster))

"He's a real turd-head." (non-thinking person)

"He's allus' gotta' chip on his shoulder, — mus' show there's wood above."

TIME

"As th' monkey with his tail cut off said, — "It won't be long now."" (humorous saying for, — it will happen very soon)

"It went on from hell ta breakfust." (lasted a very long time)

"Why, I ain't seen him inna' month a' Sundays!" (have not seen him for very long time)

"That happens onc't inna' blue moon." (occurs rarely)

"I'll be there in two shake of a lambs tail." (be there quickly)

"He ain't been 'round here inna' coon's age." (has not been around in a long time)

"If there ain't no tomorrow, ther won't be no need for that." (humorous saying to put of doing something)

"Wal, that ought'a do 'til th' cows cum' home." (that should last a long time)

"I'll be there as quick as you kin say Jack Robinson." (be there quickly)

"Wal, it's better late than never."

"It wuz fast, — happened like lightnin.'"

"It came in th' nick a' time." (very timely)

"He should be here inna' jill-flickey." (should be here very soon)

"Yep, I see him ever' whip-stitch." (often, a brief interval)

"**Remember, th' early bird catches th' worm.**" (the ones most energetic have greatest chance of success)

"**It'll be many a wet n' dry day b'fore that happens agin.'** " (a long time)

"**Nope. I ain't seen him since Hector wuz a pup.**" (haven't seen him in very long time.)

TROUBLES, PROBLEMS

"**You'd better let sleepin' dogs lie.**" (don't stir up trouble)

"**It's a lot easier to dam a creek than a river.**" (easier to take care of problems when small)

"**Better an egg today than a hen tomorrow.**" (don't let problems get bigger)

"**Might as well be hung for a sheep as a goat.**" (couldn't get in any worse trouble)

"**What goes 'round, — comes 'round.**" (justice is usually served eventually)

"**You cain't unscramble an egg.**" (some things are irreversible)

"**Ain't this a fine kittle a' fish?**" (isn't this a big mess?)

"**There's a fly in th' ointment.**" (there is a problem)

"**A kite don't rise with th' wind.**" (adversity causes strength)

"**What you sow, — you reap.**" (Bible — you (or your family) will pay for your actions)

"**He's behine th' eight-ball.**" (he is in trouble)

"**We got us 'nough trouble 'thout borryin' it.**" (don't go looking for trouble)

"**Only th' spoon that stirs th' pot knows its troubles.**" (only the ones involved know the problems)

"**I'm caught 'tween a rock anna' hard place.**" (I am trapped in a bad situation)

"**He's got his tit caught in th' wringer on that deal.**" (he's in a bad situation)

"**Wal, you cain't fall outta' a well.**" (it can't get worse, — only better)

"**Wal, that shore put a rock thru' my window!**" (that was a setback for me!)

"**He wooled me 'round like a dog with a bone.**" (he treated me pretty badly)

"**I cud'n't leave him inna' tight.**" (he was in difficulty, I had to help him)

"**Don't throw a rock inna' wasps nest.**" (don't agitate and cause more trouble)

"**Don't trouble trouble 'til trouble troubles you.**" (old saying, — don't look for trouble, it generally will come to you)

"**Ain't it funny?, — th' worst trouble don't git here.**" (many things we worry about don't happen)

"**Th' fat's in th' fire now.**" (it is big trouble now)

"**Outta' th' fryin' pan, — into th' fire.**" (out of one problem and into a bigger one)

"**Don't go pokin' up a hornets nest.**" (don't start trouble)

"**You'll just cut off yore nose to spite yer' face.**" (you will rue taking that action)

"**Don't advertise yer' troubles, — there ain't no market for'em.**"

"**I'm tellin' you, I gotta' peck a' trouble.**" (I have lots of troubles)

"**Wal, we're all in th' same boat.**" (we are in this trouble together)

"**Don't git a splinter in yer' career as you slide down th' banister of life.**"

"**Don't ever wake a sleepin' dog.**" (don't stir up trouble)

"**You'll find that life just ain't all beer an' pretzels.**" (life has its troubles)

"**Don't let th' seeds spoil yer' enjoyin' th' melon, — just spit out th' seeds!**" (shake off troubles, — enjoy life)

"**You cain't keep trouble outta' yer' house, but you don't hafta' give it a chair to sit on!**" (don't let troubles domininate you)

WEATHER, NATURE

"**That wuz a log-roller 'n toad-choker we had las' night.**" (a very hard and heavy rain)

"**It came a toad strangler on Wednesday.**" (it came a very hard & heavy rain)

"**Th' weather's dry as a goat's butt in March.**"

"**We're shore gittin' a duck drownder.**" (a very heavy rain)

"**We had us a "whip-poor-will"rain las' night.**" (we had a heavy rainstorm)

"**It rained cats 'n dogs in th' middle of th' night.**" (heavy rain)

"**It reelly rained, — like a cow pee'n onna rock.**" (a very heavy rain)

"**It did rain, — ground wuz too thick to drink, an' too thin to plow.**" (humorous saying)

WORTH, USEFULNESS

"**That (or He) ain't worth half a rats ass.**"

"**She's worth her weight in gold.**" (she is very valuable)

"**Thet shore beats a dry hackin' cough.**" (humorous saying, — that is much better than nothing)

"**She's a real gem!**" (she is very valuable)

"**His check's as good as gold.**" (has plenty of funds in bank to cover)

"**He ain't worth his salt.**" (lazy or inept, not earning his pay)

"**I wud' take that with a grain a' salt.**" (I wouldn't put much stock in that)

"**That ain't worth a hill a' beans.**" (it is worthless to me)

"**That shovel's wore out, it ain't worth two bits.**" (very little value)

"**You don't know th' worth of water 'til th' well runs dry.**" (don't appreciate something until you lose it)

"**A bird in hand is a dern sight safer'n one overhead.**" (humorous saying to mean — be satisfied, don't take chances for more)

"**You cain't beat that with a switch.**" (very good)

"**That (or he/she) ain't no slouch.**" (has good value, or good at what they do)

"**That ain't too shabby.**" (that is very satisfactory)

"**He ain't worth th' powder it'd take to blow his brains out.**"

"**She ain't worth th' powder it'd take to blow her nose!**"

"**He's th' kinda' feller you'd find in "Who's He?"**" (unknown)

"**That'll make 'bout as much diff'runce as a fart inna' tornado!**" (will have no effect whatsoever)

"**Yer' 'bout as useless as a hog with a side-saddle.**" (extremely useless)

"**That's as useless as puttin' a milk bucket under a bull.**" (a waste of time and effort)

"**It's as worthless as tits onna' boar hawg.**" (extremely worthless)

"**That's 'bout as handy as hip pockets onna' shroud.**" (no use for that)

"**I need that 'bout as much as a tomcat needs a marriage license.**" (no need for that)

"**That's as useless as two buggies inna' one-horse town.**" (very useless)

"**That's like spittin' into th' wind.**" (a wasted effort that you will regret)

"**He's worth 'bout as much as a pinch of sour owl manure.**" (he's really no good)

"**That ain't worth dried spit.**" (absolutely of no value whatsoever)

"**That knife is so dull it wud'n't cut hot butter.**"

"**That's as useless as bumps onna' side a' bacon.**" (no value)

"**That's as useless as whitewashin' horse manure, then settin' it on end.**"

"**That's as useful as a screen door onna' submarine.**" (no use whatsoever)

"**That kinda' talk is useless, — 'bout like hollerin' down a rain-barrel.**"

"**That's as useless as drawin' pictures in th' water.**"

"**That's like stoppin' th' clock to save time.**" (a wasted effort)

"**That knife is so dull, you cud' ride to town on it.**"

BOOKS BY LES BLAIR

Beyond Thyme: Herbs, Spices and "Stuff"

Gettysburg…the beginning of the end.

Ha Ha Tonka – Land of the Laughing Water

Jest Talk

Ma's Cookin'

Mom's Cookin'

Old As Dirt – So What!

Peace 'n' Plenty

South of the Border – Tex-Mex Cookin'

Talkin' Dirty

Note: The cookbooks are all different. There are no duplications in any of these books. You'll enjoy them all. Please order by contacting Ozark-Maid Candies.

Ozark-Maid Candies
5857 Osage Beach Parkway
Osage Beach, Missouri 65065
1-573-348-2202
ozarkmaid@gmail.com